Orders of Affection

Also by Arthur Smith

Elegy on Independence Day

Orders of Affection

poems by

Arthur Smith

Carnegie Mellon University Press

Pittsburgh 1996

ACKNOWLEDGMENTS

Acknowledgment is made to the following publications for poems that originally appeared in them:

Crab Orchard Review ("Late Century Ode for the Common Dead"); Crazyhorse ("A Little Death," "After Dinner with a Beautiful Woman, I Wade into the Rolling Tennessee," "Here" under the title "Whatever Light," "Sea of Blessings" under the title "The Sea of Blessings Is Beyond Measure," "Lucky," "Bad Bells," and "Isle of Palms"); The Georgia Review ("Childhood" and "Ordinary Crambles"); The Gettysburg Review ("Every Night as I Prayed God Would Kill You"); Great Stream Review ("Bad Luck"); Indiana Review ("Beauty," "Bliss," and "Happy Little Love Poem"); The Iowa Review ("In the Absence of Love, There Are Engines"); The Kenyon Review ("Kudzu in Winter," "Once in Ohio," and "Labor Day"); The Missouri Review ("The Recital" and "Untitled Canvas"); MSS ("Her Shoes"); The Nation ("Son's Blues"); New England Review ("Outdoor Theater," "End of the Line," and "Harmony"); The New Yorker ("The Least of Things" and "The Light of Being Winded"); The North American Review ("The River at Land's End"); The Pennsylvania Review ("Dull Tugs"); Poetry ("Winter Annuals"); The Southern Review ("One Life").

"Outdoor Theater" won the Poetry Society of America's Consuelo Ford Award in 1986.

"A Little Death" was selected to appear in The Pushcart Prize, XIII, 1988.

"Late Century Ode for the Common Dead" was originally titled "Tennessee Suite." It is the bicentennial ode of the University of Tennessee, 1794-1994.

Thanks are due to the Graduate School of the University of Tennessee for a research grant for the summer of 1988, during which time some of these poems were written. Thanks also to the Department of English, University of Tennessee, for a research grant for the summer of 1989, when a number of the poems in this collection were written or begun, and for a similar grant for the summer of 1991.

Special thanks to David Kitchel, Al and Jeanne Braselton, Michael Starry, Chip Delffs, Grace Schulman, David Baker, Dorothy Scura, DeWayne Rail, Al and Debbie Greco, Conrad and Beth Discont, John and Marta Gray.

Publication of this book is supported by grants from the National Endowment for the Arts in Washington, D.C., a Federal agency, and from the Pennsylvania Council on the Arts.

Library of Congress Catalog Card Number 95-067962
ISBN 0-88748-222-8
ISBN 0-88748-223-6 Pbk.

10 9 8 7 6 5 4 3 2 1

CONTENTS

This book is for Margaret

and for my sister Karen,
at whose recital the ordering began.

OUTDOOR THEATER

Given the storm bands fanning
The gulf coast,
Only one interpretation was possible.
The year was 1485, early evening.
We were witnessing the last of
The Plantagenets, Richard III, of whom
Thomas More reported,
"He came into the world feet forward,"
And was also "not untoothed."
His fiancée Lady Anne called him—
Even as he wooed her—
"A lump of foul deformity, a hedgehog,"
While his mother denounced him
As "a toad."

No wonder he was hamming it up
And, smaller wonder yet,
Bellowing and strutting,
His make-up glue loosened in the swelter
And his drooping mustache—with every line delivered—
Flagged out like a windsock
Stuffed with hair.
He was up against not only Providence,
But a squall line's lightning
And rain flung up under the A-frame sun roof,
The roof leaks streaming,
And everyone, all of us,
Outshouted by the thunder.

Later, when he was stripped to his deformities
And, like a grain sack, slung over
A horse's back and borne away for burial,
We were heartened by what we thought
Was justice, though he never
Had a chance, not a moment
When he might have reconsidered,
When, in the privacy of being
Fitted for armor, surrounded by an attendant crew,
He might have cried "Enough!"
And wandered off into the night,
No longer unrelievedly evil,
But so suddenly like us
He couldn't be sure
If the watch-fires on the outlying hills
Were sputtering
Or flaring through the rain.

Or if they were watch-fires.

KUDZU IN WINTER

Nothing as dead as, dead-beat,
Beaten back—vines like pylons
Limb to limb, rigging

On a ghost ship, the dead and living
Webbed as far as the eye can see—
Fog on the hills, and netted pines,

And a few stumps like dock pilings
After the dock's rotted and the engines
Everywhere have blown and the heat's

Seeped out and is gone, the silence
Louder than the engines ever were.
—And whatever being right had to do

With anything, and whatever beauty,
What on earth made me think it wouldn't be
Just like this at the heart of winter—

Everything not bitten back burned
With cold, and everything not burned
With the cold feeding from it?

BEAUTY

It's true the lights
As far as you and I could see
Were kicked out by the storm,
And the room grew colder by the hour—
3 or 4 a.m., I lay beside you,
And you were beautiful
In the washed-out, lamp-like light of the moon,
Just as I'd found you beautiful earlier
Walking the river bank, and even earlier
In the morning's light, harsh,
Over coffee and toast.

What with longing and apprehension,
Was it beautiful, whether
I dreamed it or had to
Think of it as a dream—that earlier
As we drowsed, I heard the dog in the hallway
And, opening the door, found her
Wide-eyed and tongue-lolling and wheezing,
And when I tried to work the dead air
Free, it was no go?

It was me, finally,
Putting as much of my mouth
Around her muzzle as I could,
And blowing as often and hard
And long as I could,
And the dog couldn't
Come around,
And there I was, naked,
My whole body throbbing—

Was that, then, something of
The beautiful, to be kneeling on the floor
And weeping, and you joining in,
Each of us holding the other,
Rocking on our knees,
The dead thing still warm between us?

THE RECITAL

Twice, in dreams,
In the ferocity of childhood,
I hacked my sister up so horribly
She's still, to this day, benefiting
From my guilt,
Though I think she had my number
Early on, long before the dreams,
About the same time she acquired
The social grace of the accordion.

What can I say, offering—
As an only brother could—
To be her one companion, doggedly encouraging
As she went rummaging through
The known musical notes
For the better part of a year,
And also to carry the contraption—bulky,
An embarrassment—to and from
Her weekly lessons?
I can almost weep
Remembering all the renditions
Of "Home on the Range" I suffered through
Between the ages of eight and nine,
And how they crippled, forever,
Whatever sense of melody
I may have had.

And yet I say Amen to all that,
And likewise to the afternoon
Of her recital—the summer heat doubling

Off the asphalt lot and pulsing
At the stained-glass windows as though
It wanted in.
There we sat, in pews,
Dressed up and miserably chilled
Whenever the air-conditioner kicked on,
Its bass-note joining the racket
In which my sister, decked out
In pinafore and ringlets,
Played no small part.

It was bad.
I was only nine
And would twice later dreamily
Do her in, but even then, wishing
I'd been brought up in an orphanage,
I was feeling the strangest order
Of affection for the girl being
Manhandled by an accordion.

It wasn't love, and we had
Shared too much
For friendship.
And then it struck me
We were "blood," that curious word
Grownups used as an excuse
For someone's failings,
As in, "Well, blood will out,"
Or, more simply, "He's blood-kin, you know,"
With the stress on "you know."

Otherwise, other
Than the blood, my sister and I
Were girl and boy, no more than strangers
Coincidentally whirled
Into an orbit
Not of our desire or design,
But thrown together thrashing,
The same way the wounded notes were then thrashing
Toward silence,
The same way everything moves
Toward silence—awkwardly, together.

ONE LIFE

This one happened to be
Siamese, on its back
On the front balcony steps,
And this time I stopped
And was combing its belly
Like a wheat field swept
Back and forth by a storm,
And it was still rippling
As it squirmed off
The planking
Two stories up.

That's when
I thought of you—
Not that instant—
There was first of all
Its one claw raking
To the step's edge
And over, a silence followed
By its breaking
Through the shrubs below,
And a moment until
It puzzled a way out,
Staring full ahead.

That's
When you came to mind,
And I can't say why.

I had thought
The cat was you—
Its willfulness and spite,
Its too affectionate address,
Though it may be I was
The one falling
Before you happened by—
Yours, simply, the one face
I stared back up into with any longing
As I sailed out of
That life.

THE LIGHT OF BEING WINDED

A curious phrase, "coming around,"
As though waking were a matter
Of lapping a track, of starting out
Full-winded and foolish,
And arriving, finally, full circle,
Back at the blocks, breathless
And seeing things in the light of being winded.

So I find myself
Sitting slump-shouldered
On the bed's edge.

Toward forty,
I'm more like my father
Than I thought I could survive.
He must have feared for me,
The way I tried his patience, the way I never seemed
To get things right.
Here, he would point, thundering,
This is Shinola.

A dozen times or more,
Over the same yellowing clumps of lawn
Watered by hand, the mosquitoes and I
Whining in what must have seemed
Like bitter clouds, I pestered him
For the details of a story,
Itself cloudlike and bitter both now
And in the winter of '35 when he was seventeen,
Hauling coal from Allentown to Jersey,
The last run till Monday,
Depending on the weather.

He was, he said, no longer in love
With the stars, or with the vista
And its whiteness and, from it,
The glare blinding. He was
Half-asleep and trucking for a living—
Tooth and ratchet, claw—gears grinding,
Wheeling down a mountainside,
Brakes giving in the rig ahead.

Following through the curves, sledding,
His own brakes pumped so hot he felt a fire
Roaring through the floorboard,
He levelled out from the cedars
And there it was, as he must have feared,
Just past a hairpin, the rig dumped,
Motor oil boiling on the block,
And the smoke, like ground mist or snow,
Swirled this way and that by the wind.

Over the years, so much of the story
Known by heart, it must have become
My heart, it must have been a dream
I'd been there with him
All along, comforted, some,
By understanding what to do
When nothing's to be done—
Stood there, chilled, overlooking the scene,
Before walking on down to the wreckage.

EVERY NIGHT AS I PRAYED GOD WOULD KILL YOU

Every night as I prayed God would kill you
In my heart, and every morning
The moment I awoke,
And all the day between,
For twelve months, one full year, I ached for you,
And then it stopped.

Not, of course,
All at once, and not as though, overnight,
The weeping willow bleeding leaves
Near the bedroom window
Were more vibrant, or the scent of hyacinths
Bunched in the planter
More coy than cloying.

The Tennessee did not surrender
Its river of coins, though it seemed
The morning light, rising, rocked on them,
Firing everywhere at once.

Nor did the animals approach me,
Heads lowered, with their solace.

Almost daily I walked the river bank,
Up and back, facing
The stark bluffs on the south shore
Where you lived,
And, one by one, I must have thrown
Half the pebbles
On the north shore into the middle.

The river pleased me, somehow—
The shore water simmered by fry and, farther out,
Small mouth churning the surface,
And powerboats plowing, and driftwood—
Bony knees knocking in the cove—
Gone the next day when I returned—
Come and gone
And coming around again
Like everything else,
With all the glitter and dazzle
And tedium and triviality, the hoopla and shouting,
And all the waste, especially the waste,
From which beauty wells.

That's when
It stopped enough for me to see
The tree leaves bathed in light,
And the feisty bluegill butting heads,
And, like plucked strings, the sprung cattails
Thrumming in the river's wash,
And a variable wind, and, over it all,
A fine mist that both soothes
And, bit by bit, erodes—small comfort,
This cooling off, this bearing down,
This wearing away.

HERE

If meaning is the reason for mournfulness,
I'm happy camping in the crowded restaurant,
Nursing decaf—bitter and oily—
As one of the Sunday dusks fronting
The end of the century
Unwinds in late springtime, Tennessee.

Outside, the yellow mums quake in the wind,
And, while the willows weep and bow,
Evening seeps into the booth beside me.
I have no thoughts, and I long for
Nothing, other
Than being party to the light,
Which has come a long way to be here,
If only for a moment,
Married to the shadows.

I'm no longer frightened
When I think of the scene without me—
Tomorrow, or forty years from now
As though it were tomorrow—
Waitresses, young and rushing, bussing trays,
Men ringing the counter, talking as they eat,
Women arrayed in booths,
Children squalling,
And, in my seat, someone else.

That's fair,
And fair's a far better deal
Than I have any right to, though that's a lesson
Harder learned than said.

I've been watching one dove
Hopping in a dogwood
Branch by branch
Toward another, the other
Branch by branch retreating.
I can't know its thoughts,
But there appears to be no sadness
In the one eye I can see,
Only the edge
Of whatever light is left
As it glances away, and then flies off
Over my head, which is the ceiling past which
I can't see.

SON'S BLUES

Earlier that evening, when the heat eased up
And red dust more powdery than flour drifted down,
Sifted through the day
By what breezes there were,

When the air was so hushed
You could hear cottonstalks drying
And weeds unfurling their new growth in the dark,
Another sound carried out over the fields.

It was like being in church, but better—
The old man there, on the porch, rocking
And drunk, and playing his guitar, coaxing out
All the wails and moans

The heart would make
If it could make such sounds
And live. I was at the window, waiting for you,
Looking out on the yard—

Toys broken and scattered
Over the hard knuckles of bermuda,
The long white runners leaking away
Almost bladeless, so intent on getting on with things.

And then the clouds crowded up, and for a long time
All I could hear was that low frying sound
A light rain makes.
It was there, insistent, as you hurried up the walk,
    laughing, your face misted with it,

And when I kissed you I could hear it,
And under your breathing my name
And the scent of your hair filling my mouth as we lay
    together, stilled,
You sleeping and the rain long ended, I could hear it,
    it was there.

BAD LUCK

Worse than bad luck, you were
Bad news. You turned out
To be the bad penny
I'd always feared—
The freezer dumped in a field, rusting and smug,
A beacon for children. Your motto must have been
A storm in every port. You might have thought
Me worse.

With us, sometimes,
It had been good, but mostly
Not. Mostly the days were
Seeded with defeat,
Like the maple out the window—
Dozens of leaf bunches clustered,
The palm-shaped, shiny leaf-blades
Reaping the sun,
And, every day, those seeds whirling
To the porch
And tracked in,
Onto the kitchen linoleum—
Fat chance.

I had just swept, bagging them
With all the other trash,
When you turned up, wanting—what?—
To see, I guess, if I were
Still in thrall.
Not with two years driven in

Between us, I wasn't,
Though after you left—
If I'd let it—some part
Of me would
Have wanted you again.
You had every right
To think so.

I was, after all, a man
Who let a woman happen to him
The same way time occurs
On a mountainside
He finds himself tramping up—
Pulled, he thinks,
By honeysuckle trumpeting
The scented fogs of summer,
While behind him a smoke-haze
Layers up the slope,
Filtering through the pines,
And the firebombers in the valley
Doze in hangars, and the next thing
You know, he's history.

LUCKY

I was so nuts back there
I barely outwitted
What must have been
Two witless state troopers
At a truck stop city
On I-40 west
Of Knoxville.
She and I
Had been at it—
Dishes thrown,
And oaths,
Her cat coiled
Behind the loveseat,
And I sped off—
I'd already been down
And would have just as well
Been dead—me crazy
With her, and her
Just crazy,
And when I managed
To shake both
Her and the law,
I thought I was lucky
Until the driver's side
Wiper flew off
And the rocker arm carved
A white arc
On the glass,
And I had to pull over
And watch them—drivers
With luck heading home,

And my home driving me
To the kind of luck
We make for ourselves,
And all of it coming
From blows in the dark,
The first of things,
Sitting out the rain
In the rain.

END OF THE LINE

I gave my mother cramps that summer,
All the way from Pennsylvania
To the central valley of California
Where I would wind up being born, in Stockton,
A place the Okies called
"End of the line."

Anyone would think so,
What with the fields
Dust-smothered by early summer
And the oleanders nodding in the heat—
Blossoms bobbing in a fitful breeze—
Mockingbirds, fluff-feathered and wing-slack,
Sprawled on the lawn—or what
Would be the lawn
If any grass were green.

And now,
A feeling of being
Drawn back, unthreaded
Through a needle—once again
Back in that backyard
Fenced with chicken wire,
And, in the sun-struck middle of the yard,
Cropping from the hardpan
And feasting on the heat,
A hornet's nest,
A honeycomb of hives.

One after another
They hatch out as I look on,
Wings stretched
And drying,
Bodies pulsing
And lifting off
For the house and the porch
And the boy unaware
On the porch, his back to me.

That's when I think
This is what it means
To witness—you can't
Help, and you can't
Go for help. It means
You'll have to see
What happens.

STILLS FROM A FILM: BLUES SINGER

1.

His head glistens, back-thrown
As though in birth, or giving birth—

What can't possibly be borne
Borne longer in saying so.

2.

Grained like wood, his face seems
Gnarled smooth, like wood rubbed

Soothingly by hands, or endlessly,
To the same end, by the sea.

LABOR DAY

Any other evening this hour
The highway banking the Tennessee
Would be channeling red stars one way
And white lights seething like the sun
The other.

I'm standing in the slow lane eastbound,
The asphalt cooling,
The air musty from it, almost sweet.
Thousands of us are gathered and gathering, milling
Or still rolling down over
The hill to the river.

A few rock
On the river in boats.

Mostly we're standing around, talking,
Though some, like me, are looking
Puzzled,
As though we had thought to find
Faces already familiar,
Instead of these, strangers
We're crowded among, all of us
Waiting for the lights flanking
The bridge to go out,
For a hush like fog over the water.

I had been looking forward
To galaxies unfurling
Overhead, to the barrage of cluster-bombs
Deafening and battering, flashes
Splintering time itself.

Now I see more clearly
Afterwards
That lull—the night
Again by streetlight and moonlight,
The tissue-thin ash drifting
And falling around us,
Like us,
Dust with a memory
As long as it falls.

And the deliberate
Climb back
Up the hillside,
Leaning into it, not talking,
Or lowly, leaning
To be heard.

DULL TUGS

Already, around a corner
Of the wharf, a block or more away,
In warehouses so empty

They're sullen, like me, in broad daylight,
Her steps echo and fade. I can no more
Go after her

Than I can hold my breath
For hours, bluing
By degrees, or walk in over my head

Into the trash-strewn, mud-churned
Channel water below. I grew up
Believing in the purity

Of commerce, thinking all of it
Occurred in books, like magic in childhood,
Or in class reports on India, Brazil,

The phrases needing only once
To be intoned—balance of trade,
Per capita, chief export—

And whatever we hungered for
Appeared—coffee and chocolate and sugar,
Ours for the having—

Nothing at all
Like the long line of arrested freighters
Backed-up

In the bay, ugly and gray
And riding low in the water, waiting to be
Maneuvered in.

BAD BELLS

Earlier, washing himself,
    his hands lathered,
Rinsing, turning over
    what she'd said about
His not wearing
    that cologne again—

The smell was
    "bad bells"—and now, next
To her, floating, those words
    echoing—as spring would,
He was sure, if all its greens, emerging,
    sounded their various notes—

And calling up others
    from a narrative unending,
Unbegun. It happened, outside,
    to be spring, and the forsythia's
Buttering wands were so vibrant
    they hurt her, though she was past

Drifting, asleep, in love with
    spring and the country
And tired of both. She'd had
    a bad time, and he had, too,
And he was trying
    to waken from his

When he turned then
    and held her, firmly, gesture
As imperative—Come with me—
    and her embracing him
As though whispering back, Be still,
    and again, Shh, be still.

IN THE ABSENCE OF LOVE, THERE ARE ENGINES

That first night gone, I was
Struck by noises—
The clock whirring

Dawnward in its gears,
Cicadas whirling ratchets in the trees,
The simmering approach

Of a pickup
Wheeling downtown
Over the dew-lathered asphalt.

The night dogs barked,
Woofing in a circle,
Then bayed

Toward the distant city buildings—
Offices, almost all of them, blazing and empty.
Even then I felt that reverberation,

That churning so relentless
It seemed the earth turned with it,
Or because of it.

Even then I knew
Without her breathing in sleep beside me
This was the permanence

I would turn to through the years,
Less and less in anger
Than relief.

HER SHOES

I've been awake, dreaming, this and that,
Looking back, restless, hesitant, today's affections
      tentative,

Tomorrow's ruthless.
Her knockabouts, for instance, butted up against the wall,
      as though she were here,

Measured—against her will, almost—against the doorframe.
Lately, more often than not, I find myself coming to
      in some interior—darker, by definition,

Than the drift of light allows—
Measured myself, somehow.

WINTER ANNUALS

Sometimes I think these
Were the stars
I prayed to seven years ago
While she slept beside me,
Almost calm.
Or else it was the ceiling,
Bits of mica glittering
Like fool's gold in a riverbed
I drifted down, dreamward finally,
Beyond fatigue, both of us
Easing over a wooded hillside,
The earth moss-softened and vivid
With the blossoms
We stopped for—chicory,
Cow-vetch, lupin and larkspur,
And, rare on a bank, a shooting star,
Its violet petals plumed.

When the oaks opened out,
We waded back through
A field of white asters,
Like star-sparkle on a winter's night,
And lingered over a scattering
Of snowdrops lolling
Mutely and briefly,
And, nearer home,
A leopard lily drooping as though
It longed for the tropics. Hardly
The tropics now—
Two feet of crusted snow, or more,
And the air so bitter
It can barely be breathed.

—That I could be caught
Flatfooted again in the snow, in January,
No longer chilled
But numb, the luminous bodies
Once again returned, the same ones,
Estranged by time,
Closer and clearer in the cold,
As though leaning,
The whispers almost audible—
If I stay long enough,
If I listen—
The lesson always about
To be learned.

ONCE IN OHIO

I would have done
          almost anything
Not to have had to
          see her joining me
That first time in
          the claw-footed tub
In Athens, her robe
          falling and a long
Red welt, the kind
          a bicycle chain
Can make, bristling over
          the ribs, the left
Side of her chest.
          She stood there,
And I could make out
          past her, drifting
Through the chute of light
          at the window, clusters
Of snowflakes like scraps
          of paper from a bonfire,
Lifted by their burning
          and then released.
I knew that everything
          had been changed,
And I was afraid, I was
          like a cedar fitted
For the winter with snow;
          and then she started to
Step in, and I helped her
          sit down facing me
As the water rose
          around us.

THE LEAST OF THINGS

From here, hillside, I've stopped to admire
The evening primrose—
A pink, water-colored wildflower

Brought to bloom
Only inches above ground,
Its petals so diaphanous the weeds

Green through, so fragile
Being looked at seems
To bring on its withering.

The hills, too, constantly
Revising landscape, are restless,
Or so they might appear

To someone passing through,
Though from a great height, cloud-level
And above, soaring—cirrus, we call these,

Little filaments or tufts
Of atmosphere—from great height, the earth,
In its placid demeanor, rocks.

This is what frightened Whitman:
Out of all indifferent decay
Indifferent beauty springs.

This primrose, for instance,
I've come back to,
Alluring with the surge within,

Also called a buttercup, by children,
Because it powders up their noses
With the buttery dust of germination.

Persisting, one of many, it surfaces
Through the cream-colored froth
Of meadow foam

Spilling out over the hillside,
Which, this closely, is beautified entirely
By the minions of corruption.

CHILDHOOD

That simply, that richly, the days were under way,
And I remember them, breezes

Wafting from the spice-islands of the past
Where even now the plums darken almost

Beyond desire. Almost? Well, then, beyond,
Though with what exhilaration we set sail—

Tail winds bullying the stitched canvas,
Our course determined by the stars.

Night and day we endured—the seawinds
Brackish, the repetitions tedious—

Until we anchored off an island
Never charted,

From which we expected much—
Not what we found: the bones

Of those before us, the earth disturbed,
A chest filled with nothing, the light of day.

A LITTLE DEATH

Anyone almost anywhere on the walkway
Could have heard it—I did—

That boom-like grunting
Through the late summer Sunday afternoon

Drowse of the Knoxville Zoo.
Here, I thought, was an animal so overwhelmed

The most it could hope for
Was to bellow into being that intensity—

Those waves mounting, even then bearing it away.
I joined the crowd around the tortoise pen

Where earlier, leaning over a barrier of logs
And stroking the larger of the two,

His fatherly, reptilian neck craning
Tolerantly, it seemed, I had reckoned him old,

So old, in fact, that looking back into the pen
I thought I'd find him dead or, worse, living,

But at the end. He was "dying," to be sure,
Clambered up on the other's high-humped back,

His stump-like front feet extended forward,
Grasping the female's weathered shell,

His own neck dangling, gaze floating,
And from his mouth, saliva swaying on short thick threads

Only inches from the other's bony face.
And, all along, the noise.

It wasn't pretty, though it was soon over,
What we called "makin' bacon"

Back when all knowledge belonged to the young,
Here witnessed in the frank generation of matter,

All amenities beside the fact—
The male beached on his own bulk, less tolerant

Of the heavy-handed petting,
And the female, unencumbered again,

Shuffling toward the mud-bracketed pond
Tattered with froth-pads of algae,

Immersing herself as far as
The shallow water would allow.

LATE CENTURY ODE FOR THE COMMON DEAD

1.

Not history, not the past—
I see that now—
Students on a commons stage,
Crowded and crowding back
Red-faced with bullhorns,
The San Francisco
Bay winds whipped
Colder by helicopters crossing
And re-crossing the square,
Each pendulum-like pass
Lower than the one before
And louder, a wake rolling over
Those of us stopped on
The way elsewhere,
Trying to make out
Between turbulences what was
Being said.

I'm still trying to make it out
Twenty-five years later
In Knoxville where I live,
On the campus where I work,
On the lower south side of a hill
Falling off to the Tennessee,
Just uphill
From a chestnut oak
I'm standing below.
Here, in 1901, breaking ground
For a women's hall long since lived-in
And out-lived

And razed back to the ground
It seemed to spring from,
The bodies of eight soldiers, all Union, men and boys,
        were unearthed—
A few buttons, bones,
Uniform tatters.

Now, what with the blizzard
And flooding, the dogwoods are late lifting
Their broken cups
To the sunlight working
April's inclination, the same light
Fostering the thickets after Chickamauga
And leading the buttercups there in their slow yellow
        fan across the meadows.

To my right, a van
Idling in front
Of the nuclear engineering complex,
And traffic on the bridge south,
And a tugboat's vented blast,
And behind me, the stadium,
Its pillars and girders
Weathering without sound,
As the library on my left is,
Its stories terraced,
Receding in shadows,
And in front of me, topping the hill,
The tower of the oldest building from which, now,
The cracking of a window
Going up,
A man in a white shirt
Leaning out, looking around.

2.

Once, not far from here,
Was a graveyard no one's heard of,
One of several in Dempsey Branch,
Just south of Mt. Gay
In far southwestern West Virginia.

From anywhere in it, a thrown rock
Would clear the chicken wire
Fencing in the stones
That barely last past the names—
Ballard Ellis, his wife Bessie,
Their children Clifford and Lura Belle
And Roy Lee, aged two months,
The lettering netted over
With vines, more and more difficult
To read.

The graveyard's known
As Mounts,
After the grocer
Who gave the land around the time
The killings ended farther south
Between the Hatfields and McCoys,
And just before they started up
Among the union organizers,
And the Pinkertons,
And those fierce plain folks
The coal miners
Of neighboring Matewan.

I know these things because the Ellises—
My mother's family—were buried there,
As Mounts was, until last fall
When the road from Holden
To Logan went in
And my mother's youngest sister witnessed
The exhumation of the bodies—
What passed for them—
The remains trucked
Twenty miles
To Forest Lawn Cemetery
Near Chapmanville:

Of their father,
A blue tie, she swears—
No bones, nothing
Of his coffin; of the mother,
On one of several
Fingerbones, a wedding band.

It sounds apocryphal, but
I've stood there and
Thrown a rock
Clear of it,
Out into the underbrush.
I've seen what had been given
Taken back.

When I look at the white fog
Pooling in the valleys
And the cloud-rivers
Winding thinly

Between the pitched hills,
I begin to hear from the pines
That breathing I thought of
Once as mournful, and then
As the one sound desire
Underscores the others with, and finally
As wind in the needles,
Bearing nothing,
And bearing it away.

3.

We talk about the end of the world
As though it were the end
Of the world.
We like to think
The time and place we occupy
Is central.

It is nothing to the markers
Lining the narrow circular drive
Of National Cemetery,
The headstones
Wheeling as I stop
And walk to the nearest—
Dead so long
I run my hand over the smooth-
Looking stones—
They're deeply pitted
And coarse, not comforting—

They're not supposed to be comforting,
These graves,
Men and women of whom
Nothing's known, other than
Names as common
As those I hear and say
Almost every day—
Hodges and Ayres, Holt and McClung,
Neyland and Morgan and Stokely—
On towers and stadiums,
On libraries:

Teachers' names and merchants'
And soldiers' more widely remembered,
Perhaps, than these,
But all challenged in the dailiness
Of their own beliefs, with few of them
Comforted by the pasts
They looked back to,
And none of them rescued by what was
Already known,
Though they brought what they knew as far forward
As they could
Before it became
Part of the story
Time now tells about them.

Wherever the eight are,
I can't find them.
Neither can the caretaker
Scanning the tops, wave after wave.

It's late July
As I walk back to the car,
Sweating in a drought summer,
The walnut trees bearing up,
The lawn not,
The maple leaves
Browning from the tips,
The shade afforded by them
Sweeping the day's heat along,
The headstones cooling
On either side in row on row rippling
From the center, the plots
Lettered and numbered—
D103, 102, 101—
The names on the other side,
Cut into and
Weathering back out of time:

Wm Winn, Tenn Inf,

And Robt Laferty, US Hv Arty,

And John Davis of North Carolina,

And Wm Allen, and so on.

HARMONY

The air's still vivid—
I was sipping coffee one evening,
My mind nowhere in particular,
When the phone rang, someone saying
She was dead—and I was falling after ages, it seemed,
Without a single thought of her
Piercing me.

I walked out on the porch,
The floor boards shimmering like the ghosts of boards,
And everything—the roof pillars, the swing,
The steps wooden to the walk—all slightly
Off kilter and wavering
As though I were drunk or dreaming,
Or the porch itself were dreaming
Its worst fear, flames fanned
By a summer's evening breeze
From the scorched kitchen
To the porch.

The moon seemed to be all right,
Bone-lustered and full.
It seemed to go on.
And the high-soaring fireflies had ambition,
Shorting overhead in the general mix of the stars.

One block, another—
Windows, some, lighting up
And others going black
As I went on, sometimes clear-eyed
Or dumb with loss.

—That's where the dream ended,
Me walking, having lost her twice.

I'm sitting up in bed,
Washed in moonlight and streetlight
And the filmy yellowish outdoor porchlight.
You're turned away, I can barely
Hear the cushion of your breathing.
An hour, less, since we were making love,
The sheets heaped up, curling
Like surf around waders,
And I thought, it's worth it—
Death, I mean—
Being able to love you,
And now I know what that means—
You and I in that room, rocking
With loss and love and loss.

BLISS

I was, I like to think, thought-free
Briefly, shuffling through the leaves
Scattered before me like rose petals,
The air tinged with autumn, though no
Leaf smoke yet spiced the night breeze.

Just before, I'd been somber with
The morning's coming duties—
Then the leaves occurred and I was
Brought up short, laughing with the dust
The days had sifted on my pillow.

—Kept up how many nights by wonder:
Where it falls from, from however far,
Before I learned to take my pleasure
In simplicity—knowing you were waiting,
Knowing you knew I was on the way.

HAPPY LITTLE LOVE POEM

A week ago I wondered where
It went, that lost little

Lusciousness, that first kiss
I passed up in noon heat,

The eucalyptus leaves filtering
Light on her freckled arms,

Her eyes hazel-shaded and coy, talk
Faltering, traffic and the noises

People make oblivious to kisses missed
In the park coming back into focus.

Now the curtains allowing afternoon light
The play of her down hair, glistening,

And a blush on her chest, freckled also,
And I'm kneeling, kissing her,

And she's more sugary than hard sauce
Spooned over a bowl of blackberries

Sun-swollen and warm and still ripening
As I bring them to my lips.

SEA OF BLESSINGS

Out the window, a hollyhock toppling
Under a welter of bees,
And the heart-shaped leaves of the morning glory—
Its blossoms already puckered—
Spiraling up the handle of a hoe
Propped against the chainlink fence.

Under the feeder, squabbling,
Starlings in twos and threes—
Tails bobbed, breast feathers
Grease-splattered—
Stalking stiffly, flatfooted,
As though on snowshoes, unmoved
By the downpour on their heads:
A jay on the feeder, with the side
Of its bill, shoveling birdseed over
In its own clumsy hunger.

And here I am, lazy
In the lull of sleeping past noon—
The city, and everyone in it, as far as I care,
From here on out,
Humming along without me—
Seawinds
Endlessly in off the sea
And over the coastal range.

How could I not bow
Down to it? How could
Anyone, finally, not?

ORDINARY CRAMBLES

These were not your ordinary crambles—
Boughs and branches broken by the wind.
I could tell *that* even before the storm,

By the huddled twittering and murmuring
Of starlings confused in the trees,
A din the English used to call "chirming."

So when the knee-high weeds no longer
Doddered in the wind, I edged out far enough
To find the redwood tree slit lengthwise

Toe to crown. Shuddering through the trunk,
The bolt must have frenzied the bark
And outer branches, both of which

Burst into the jagged, long-haired slivers
Littering the balcony and bangled lawn.
Meaningless, all of it,

Except for the hunger to sort significance
From the chips and tatters drifting down,
Fragments that become, unattended,

The rankness legends mushroom out of—
Incredible—or, attended to too hopefully,
Only themselves, and less.

THE RIVER AT LAND'S END

From my mother I learned
The word "specific"—not any ocean,
But that one, right out there, the Pacific—
She and I on a bridge abutment
As my father switchbacked
Down a dirt bluff,
Pole bobbing above
Manzanita branches—sticks, really,
Brittle and straggled over
With a few dust-coated leaves—
The river rapids
Frothing with the kind of danger I was
Too young for, though sunlight glistened
Like honey in the shallow pools.

Now, out the window, darkness mostly
And ground lights here and there,
Clustered and bristling,
Little rashes
Flickering almost all the way
Down to the sea. I used to be
One of those lights, I lived there,
Where the sea—if you look and listen—
Washes its hands of us
And we call it beautiful.

There are moments
Nothing can take away—not time
Or distance, though they try—
The butter-colored pop-ups
Wiry along the bluff,

Swells washing up
Just as rumpled
And bluegray as last year's,
And the river bearing itself back
Just as you are being borne back,
In course and out, down
To where the sea accepts
What was earlier given out—

Wind sanding the tips of the waves—

AFTER DINNER WITH A BEAUTIFUL WOMAN, I WADE INTO THE ROLLING TENNESSEE

OK, I'll be a fool for you, for now, head over
    and into—sung, usually,

Those things too stupid to be said, and here I am,
    living out a love letter with

Anthems in my heart—
    the clamor of you, of blade and blossom

Slick on a rumpled hillside and the river running
    high with the summer rains—

The physical world no longer
    what I bicker with

To keep back some imagined
    horror of the truth, but rather,

Every moment now with you, the moments freed and tumbling,
    and no one wistful on the bank, waving or counting.

ISLE OF PALMS

When I walked out
    this morning, muttering along
With the sea static, the breezes
    so insistent a distraction,
The waves brown and mottled
    and frothing to a stop,

And the Atlantic, as little
    as I could see, open—
Only a shrimp boat, its outriggers
    down and seining,
And Fort Sumter in the sea mist
    like a ghost island—

And after that, nothing,
    what you'd expect—the pipers
Skittish, the pelicans
    biding their time
From way back—and would've walked on
    but a thunderhead backed

Me around and
    scattered showers—
Warm, soothing, without
    intention—on my head.
You must have smiled to
    see me faster

Returning than leaving,
        trailing storm clouds
As melodramatic as any
        I could have called up
On a dare, on my own,
        as a fool, but

Didn't. Sometimes
        the right thing happens.
Sometimes you can get away
        with saying
A word like "forever,"
        even two days running.

UNTITLED CANVAS

I've been home from the gallery
Since late noon, and all this time,
While the swamp oaks have been rowing
Through the blown rain,
I've been thinking of a canvas
In which one of the masters
Lets it be known
Life is sad.

We're all there,
Working switchbacks up a mountainside
Obscured by fog, and rain falling through fog,
Our wooden carts so rickety and overloaded
There seems to be no hope,
Though the bronze and copper cart bells
Clinking all around us
Make a soothing counterpoint
To the steady growling of the wheels.
And so we go on walking, and sooner or later fall,
And the living lay us out
On the side of the road,
As we laid those
Before us,
And then set out again,
Haze lifting over a mountain
Beautifully shaped by shadows
And the seemly generations of wind and rain.

The old man knew, all right,
Sometimes it seems easier to believe
Nothing matters, though
There's a difference
Between wishing you'd never been born
And wishing you were dead.
That difference is hardly mean
When you can be laid back, as I am, in a breakfast nook,
    lingering over blackberries
So heavenly plump
You'd find it hard to believe
The earth could issue up a sweetness
So darkly beaded, scented with its own dust.

For this once,
For the first time I can think of,
I've finished off, without reservation, whatever deliciousness
    I could get my hands on,
And I'd have a hard time believing it
Myself, except
For the magenta smudges
Drying on the white bowl.

CARNEGIE MELLON POETRY

1975
The Living and the Dead, Ann Hayes
In the Face of Descent, T. Alan Broughton

1976
The Week the Dirigible Came, Jay Meek
Full of Lust and Good Usage, Stephen Dunn

1977
How I Escaped from the Labyrinth and Other Poems, Philip Dacey
The Lady from the Dark Green Hills, Jim Hall
For Luck: Poems 1962–1977, H.L. Van Brunt
By the Wreckmaster's Cottage, Paula Rankin

1978
New & Selected Poems, James Bertolino
The Sun Fetcher, Michael Dennis Browne
A Circus of Needs, Stephen Dunn
The Crowd Inside, Elizabeth Libbey

1979
Paying Back the Sea, Philip Dow
Swimmer in the Rain, Robert Wallace
Far from Home, T. Alan Broughton
The Room Where Summer Ends, Peter Cooley
No Ordinary World, Mekeel McBride

1980
And the Man Who Was Traveling Never Got Home, H.L. Van Brunt
Drawing on the Walls, Jay Meek
The Yellow House on the Corner, Rita Dove
The 8-Step Grapevine, Dara Wier
The Mating Reflex, Jim Hall

1981
A *Little Faith*, John Skoyles
Augers, Paula Rankin
Walking Home from the Icehouse, Vern Rutsala
Work and Love, Stephen Dunn
The Rote Walker, Mark Jarman
Morocco Journal, Richard Harteis
Songs of a Returning Soul, Elizabeth Libbey

1982
The Granary, Kim R. Stafford
Calling the Dead, C.G. Hanzlicek
Dreams Before Sleep, T. Alan Broughton
Sorting It Out, Anne S. Perlman
Love Is Not a Consolation; It Is a Light, Primus St. John

1983
The Going Under of the Evening Land, Mekeel McBride
Museum, Rita Dove
Air and Salt, Eve Shelnutt
Nightseasons, Peter Cooley

1984
Falling from Stardom, Jonathan Holden
Miracle Mile, Ed Ochester
Girlfriends and Wives, Robert Wallace
Earthly Purposes, Jay Meek
Not Dancing, Stephen Dunn
The Man in the Middle, Gregory Djanikian
A Heart Out of This World, David James
All You Have in Common, Dara Wier

1985
Smoke from the Fires, Michael Dennis Browne
Full of Lust and Good Usage, Stephen Dunn (2nd edition)
Far and Away, Mark Jarman
Anniversary of the Air, Michael Waters
To the House Ghost, Paula Rankin
Midwinter Transport, Anne Bromley

1986
Seals in the Inner Harbor, Brendan Galvin
Thomas and Beulah, Rita Dove
Further Adventures With You, C.D. Wright
Fifteen to Infinity, Ruth Fainlight
False Statements, Jim Hall
When There Are No Secrets, C.G. Hanzlicek

1987
Some Gangster Pain, Gillian Conoley
Other Children, Lawrence Raab
Internal Geography, Richard Harteis
The Van Gogh Notebook, Peter Cooley
A Circus of Needs, Stephen Dunn (2nd edition)
Ruined Cities, Vern Rutsala
Places and Stories, Kim R. Stafford

1988
Preparing to Be Happy, T. Alan Broughton
Red Letter Days, Mekeel McBride
The Abandoned Country, Thomas Rabbitt
The Book of Knowledge, Dara Wier
Changing the Name to Ochester, Ed Ochester
Weaving the Sheets, Judith Root

1989
Recital in a Private Home, Eve Shelnutt
A Walled Garden, Michael Cuddihy
The Age of Krypton, Carol J. Pierman
Land That Wasn't Ours, David Keller
Stations, Jay Meek
The Common Summer: New and Selected Poems, Robert Wallace
The Burden Lifters, Michael Waters
Falling Deeply into America, Gregory Djanikian
Entry in an Unknown Hand, Franz Wright

1990
Why the River Disappears, Marcia Southwick
Staying Up For Love, Leslie Adrienne Miller
Dreamer, Primus St. John

1991
Permanent Change, John Skoyles
Clackamas, Gary Gildner
Tall Stranger, Gillian Conoley
The Gathering of My Name, Cornelius Eady
A Dog in the Lifeboat, Joyce Peseroff
Raised Underground, Renate Wood
Divorce: A Romance, Paula Rankin

1992
Modern Ocean, James Harms
The Astonished Hours, Peter Cooley
You Won't Remember This, Michael Dennis Browne
Twenty Colors, Elizabeth Kirschner
First A Long Hesitation, Eve Shelnutt
Bountiful, Michael Waters
Blue for the Plough, Dara Wier
All That Heat in a Cold Sky, Elizabeth Libbey

1993
Trumpeter, Jeannine Savard
Cuba, Ricardo Pau-Llosa
The Night World and the Word Night, Franz Wright
The Book of Complaints, Richard Katrovas

1994
If Winter Come: Collected Poems, 1967–1992, Alvin Aubert
Of Desire and Disorder, Wayne Dodd
Ungodliness, Leslie Adrienne Miller
Rain, Henry Carlile
Windows, Jay Meek
A Handful of Bees, Dzvinia Orlowsky

1995
Germany, Caroline Finkelstein
Housekeeping in a Dream, Laura Kasischke
About Distance, Gregory Djanikian
Wind of the White Dresses, Mekeel McBride
Above the Tree Line, Kathy Mangan
In the Country of Elegies, T. Alan Broughton
Scenes from the Light Years, Anne C. Bromley
Quartet, Angela Ball
Rorschach Test, Franz Wright

1996
Back Roads, Patricia Henley
Dyer's Thistle, Peter Balakian
Beckon, Gillian Conoley
The Parable of Fire, James Reiss
Cold Pluto, Mary Ruefle
Orders of Affection, Arthur Smith
Colander, Michael McFee